On Dinosaur Days

Dinosaur-related hands-on learning activities

Compiled by
Sherry Burrell

Art by
Debby Dixler

FIRST TEACHER PRESS
First Teacher, Inc./Bridgeport,CT

ISBN   1-878727-00-1

Cover and Page Design: Gene Krackehl
Cover photo: Andrew Brilliant and Carol Palmer (taken at Westfield Child Center, Brockton, MA)

Editor: Martha A. Hayes
Editorial Assistants: Jessica Rubenstein, Alicia La-France, Thomas Jenen
Art Editor: Debby Dixler
Computer Graphics: Jill Levine
Typesetting and Layout: Anita Golton, Jeffrey Goldfarb
Manufactured in the United States of America

Special thanks to Lisa Schustak, Hillary and Scott Dixler, and Jennifer Durkin.

Published by First Teacher Press, First Teacher, Inc.
P.O. Box 29, 60 Main Street, Bridgeport, CT 06602

ON DINOSAUR DAYS was inspired by the many creative ideas in "Dinosaur Days," an issue of First Teacher magazine (Volume 11, No. 2, February, 1990) I owe many thanks to the following contributing authors: Donna Bird, Ellen Javernick, Kathleen Koons, Terry Jeffers Moore, Judith Nuss, Eileen Patch, Jeannine Perez, Catherine Reeves, Karin-Leigh Spicer, Jean Stangl.

Illustrator Debby Dixler has again managed to bring a manuscript alive with her clear and lively drawings. I am also grateful to Lisa Durkin for her patience and faith in my abilities. Happy Dinosaur Days to You! S. B.

TABLE OF CONTENTS

• All bulleted pages are reproducible.

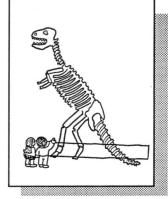

The thought that at one time a creature as huge and threatening as a dinosaur could have roamed the earth fascinates our young children. Dinosaurs have an appeal for little people because dinosaurs are signs of power and strength to them. When you are small enough to walk under a table and feel you have very little to say about most decisions, power and might are important.

Learning about dinosaurs and playing with dinosaur figures captivates a child's imagination. Through play, children begin to gain control over their excitement and fear. Children's self esteem is automatically enhanced as they feel powerful and independent playing with and talking about these sometimes gigantic and fierce creatures who lived so very long ago.

It does not take much effort to get children to talk about dinosaurs. Pre-schoolers are so fascinated with dinosaurs that the subject naturally encourages all kinds of language opportunities. But because dinosaurs are such a popular topic, it is easy for young children to pick up common misconceptions about them. For example, although it is not known what colors dinosaurs were, models of them must be made in one color or another. For this reason, children may be "sure" that the Apatosaurus/Brontosaurus was actually green! It is important to find out what children already think they know about dinosaurs so that accurate information can replace any misconceptions.

The subject of dinosaurs can lend itself to any part of the curriculum. Using dinosaurs adds creativity and excitement to topics that otherwise might have seemed dreary and un-impressive to our youngsters. There is something about the "terrible lizards" that intrigues us all.

How to Use this Book

This book is presented as a comprehensive system of activities, all drawing from the single theme of dinosaurs. If you are planning a dinosaur unit, consider these tips:

- Determine what you and your children already know.
- Read up on the latest, most accurate facts.
- Check out available resources and collect materials.
- Plan to spend enough time on the topic.
- Make facts meaningful to children.
- Provide activities in every curricular area.
- Offer both teacher-directed and child-directed activities.
- Foster imagination and have fun!

Patterns

The heavily outlined dinosaur patterns in this book have been especially designed to make them easy for young learners to cut out. Though each pattern accompanies a specific activity, each one can be used interchangeably with most of the pattern related activities.

As you and your children are going through the activities in this book, the following facts about dinosaurs can be used as discussion springboards. As you continue to explore dinosaurs, compile your own facts checklist, adding to the list as you unearth more and more information.

Remember too, that scientists are discovering more about dinosaurs all the time. Be sure that what you impart to children about dinosaurs is accurate and up-to-date.

Checklist of Facts

❑ There are no dinosaurs living now, they are extinct. Dinosaurs died out 65 million years ago, long before people ever existed, and are called prehistoric animals.

❑ Extinct means "died out." Many people believe that dinosaurs became extinct because the world got too hot; others believe the world became too cold. For six theories of extinction, see *Life and Death of Dinosaurs* by Pascal Chenel (Barron's Educ. Series).

❑ During the time that dinosaurs roamed the earth, various species lived and died out during those 150 million years.

❑ Other prehistoric animals that have become extinct include the following: mastodons, giant beavers, mammoths, giant ground sloths, and saber-toothed cats. Today, certain species that are in danger of becoming extinct include the following: tree sloths, mountain gorillas, orangutans, rhinos, tigers, some whales, and bison.

❑ Some animals in existence today like species of turtles, crocodiles, cockroaches, starfish, and jellyfish also lived during the time of the dinosaurs.

❑ In the earliest dinosaur era (Triassic), the continents of the earth were mostly one big mass (everything was connected together). By the time the dinosaurs became extinct, the continents had separated from each other and were close to the positions they are today.

❑ Not all dinosaurs were huge. Some were the size of chickens or cats.

❑ No one knows what color dinosaurs were or what noises they made. Scientists believe the skin of dinosaurs may have displayed many different colors and patterns.

❑ Brontosaurus has recently been renamed Apatosaurus. At first when they studied various bones that had been found, scientists thought these were two different species of dinosaur. But in 1979, when the skull was found, they realized they were both the same. Since Apatosaurus was the name first given to the bones, it is now this dinosaur's official name.

❑ Some children might have models of Dimetrodon and call it a dinosaur. This prehistoric creature had a sail, like Spinosaurus, but it was NOT a dinosaur. It was an early mammal-like reptilian lizard that lived before the Triassic Period.

❑ Some children may have models of Pteranodon (te-RAN-uh-don) "winged and toothless lizard." This prehistoric creature was NOT a dinosaur. Its wingspan was up to 27' and it weighed only 20 pounds. It lived near the sea and ate fish during the late Cretaceous Period.

Books

• *The Rourke Dinosaur Dictionary* by Joseph Hincks (Rourke) Written for use by older children and adults, this picture dictionary includes dinosaur groups and time lines. A glossary includes the alphabetical picture and description listings for many dinosaurs. Each listing provides general statistics about size, weight, time periods, and location of the fossils found. The oversized picture dictionary can be used by small children for "looking".

• *Dinosaurs and Other Extinct Animals* by Gabriel Beaufay (Barron's Education Series) An extremely detailed book that explains what life forms preceded the dinosaur and what kinds of creatures followed them when they died out. It is a complete "mini course" which will fill in the gaps for educator comprehension.

• *Life and Death of Dinosaurs* by Pascal Chenel (Barron's Educational Series) A book for the teachers' own collection! This wonderful little book is big on fact, covering everything from the history of dinosaur findings, to egg laying habits, to six of the theories of extinction.

• *What Happened to the Dinosaurs* by Franklyn Branley (Crowell) An excellent resource which can be shared with children. Help children compare what happened to the dinosaurs with what is happening today to endangered species.

Sources For Classroom Materials

• Children's Book and Music Center 2500 Santa Monica Blvd, Santa Monica, CA 90904. Telephone number: 213-829-0215. Catalog

offerings include dinosaur storybooks and recordings such as "Dynamic Dinosaurs" (introduces eleven dinosaurs with an accompanying booklet of fingerplays, skills, and phonics activities), and "Once Upon a Dinosaur" (features such songs as "Fossil Rock" and "My Pet Tyrannosaurus," as well as an activity guide).

• Insect Lore Products P.O. Box 1535 Shafter, CA 93263. Telephone number: 805-746-6047. A supplier of science and nature study materials, books, and videotapes. This company offers all kinds of dinosaur study materials appropriate for early learning. Catalogue offerings include: crepe puzzles, wooden dino skeleton kits, a claymation video, and a remarkable dinosaur board game.

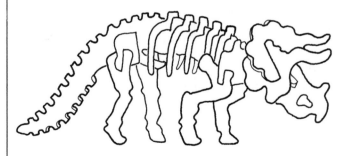

• Dover Publications 31 East Second Street, Mineola, NY 11501. Looking for fine quality full color posters of dinosaurs? Dover offers one free with every two posters purchased. They also offer dinosaur cut-and-use stencils, iron-on transfers, directions for making stuffed dinosaurs, skeleton models, stickers, seals, coloring books, and ready-to-frame dinosaur paintings.

DINOSAUR FACTS:
- Scene from Cretaceous Period; Tyrannosaurus Rex is attacking a Triceratops; in background, Spinosaurus is searching for meat and Ankylosaurus is hiding in undergrowth; Pteranodon in the sky is gliding, not flying.

What You'll Need:
Copies of page 9 • crayons or markers • scissors • oaktag • large chart paper • tape recorder.

Introduction:
As an introductory activity for your dinosaur unit, ask children what they know, or think they know, about dinosaurs. Tape record the discussion and later write the ideas given by children on an experience chart. Then, at the close of the dinosaur unit, ask children to tell you what they have learned about dinosaurs from the activities and stories. Once again, record their responses on a chart. Help children compare the two experience charts.

What to Do:
1. Give each child, or show the group a copy of page 9. Have children describe what they see in the picture. Use this discussion as a springboard for further discussions of dinosaurs.
2. Ask questions about dinosaurs and accept all answers. Following are some questions you can use to start your discussions or to broaden children's thinking about dinosaurs.

   "Were dinosaurs real or pretend?"
   "What did dinosaurs eat?"
   "When did they live?"
   "What are some kinds of dinosaurs?"
   "What happened to dinosaurs?"
   "What sizes were dinosaurs?"
   "What is a fossil?"
   "What is a skeleton?"
   "Why did dinosaurs die?"

   "What did (<u>name of type of dinosaur</u>) look like?"
   "What different body coverings did dinosaurs have?"
   "Did all the different dinosaurs live at the same time?"
   "Did any other animals live at the same time as dinosaurs?"
   "What might have happened if the dinosaurs hadn't died?"
   "What might happen if a real dinosaur visited today?"
3. Let children color their discussion pictures if they wish.

Challenges:
- Encourage children to discover more about one creature in the picture. Have each child focus on that creature when doing other activities throughout the unit.

Making Connections:
- Have children bring from home any dinosaur books, models, stuffed animals, toys, or games related to prehistoric times. Help children use the objects to make a display table. Have the owners tell about their items at appropriate times during the unit.

Books and Resources:
Patrick's Dinosaurs by Carol Carrick (Clarion Books)

Set Up A Dinosaur Learning Center

1. Designate a space in your room, and put up a dinosaur-shaped sign (use pattern) saying "DINO MANIA"!
2. Gather as many of the materials listed below as you can find, and display them in a corner for Dino Mania. Choose materials that present accurate portrayals of what dinosaurs were really like.
3. Invite the children to bring in dinosaur items from home.
4 Locate (or make) as many of the following items as you can (with a dinosaur theme, of course):

stickers	cookie cutters
stencils	recordings
books	posters
figures	skeletons
awards/buttons	mobiles
inflatables	costumes
masks	puppets
lotto/table games	puzzles
models	bandaids
food items	stuffed animals
bookmarks	games
clothes items	filmstrips
videos	flannel items
bulletin board items	

Classroom Management

Since children naturally seem fascinated by dinosaurs, why not consider using a few of the following ideas as aids in classroom management:

● Classroom chores take dinosaur names: Cleanosaurus, Tablesettingosaurus, Plantcarosaurus, Leaderosaurus, Pickuposaurus. Make badges with the long titles and present them to the helpers.

● Help each child trace around his foot and cut out the print. Have the child write his name on the print and add the letters "osaurus" (Kevinosaurus). Use these footprints (or personalized dinosaur shapes) as signs for the children's cubby spaces, chairs, cots or attendance charts.

● The class trash barrel can be used as a way to "feed the dinosaur". Tape a huge outline of a dinosaur (Use an enlarged pattern.) the children have decorated onto the trash bin. Maybe this dino could be called Trashosaurus!

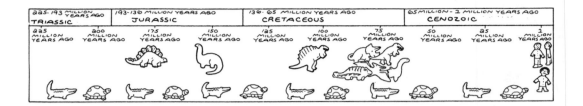

225-193 MILLION YEARS AGO	193-136 MILLION YEARS AGO	136-65 MILLION YEARS AGO	65 MILLION-2 MILLION YEARS AGO
TRIASSIC	JURASSIC	CRETACEOUS	CENOZOIC

What You'll Need:

Shelf paper • Dinosaur Patterns • construction paper • scissors • crayons or markers • tape.

Introduction:

Dinosaurs dominated the earth for more than 150 million years--from 225 to 65 million years ago, during the Mesozoic Era. Humans have only existed for the past one million years. About one hundred fifty to two hundred years ago the first dinosaur fossils were found. However, all the fossils found were from dinosaurs that had died more than 65 million years ago.

It is difficult for young children to deal with the concept of how long ago dinosaurs lived because these prehistoric creatures' bones are still being found <u>today</u>. They need to understand that dinosaurs died out <u>long</u> before any people were born--before their grandparents, before the Pilgrims, before the Native Americans, even before the first cave dwellers.

Sometimes children think all the different kinds of dinosaurs lived at the same time. Actually, some were separated by millions of years. Here is an activity to show this.

What to Do:

1. Put a long piece of shelf paper horizontally along a wall to use as a time line. Write from left to right the numbers in millions at the top of the chart from 225 million to 1 million. Use increments of 25 million years so you have ten numbers. As you continue through these directions, add the numbers listed in their approximate positions.

2. Have ready or let children help cut out paper shapes of people, turtles, crocodiles, Tyrannosaurus Rex, Triceratops, Spinosaurus, Ankylosaurus, Stegosaurus, Plesiosaurus, Pteranodon, and Apatosaurus (Brontosaurus). Use the patterns in this book for different dinosaurs.

3. At the right-hand edge of the time line—1 million years—help children attach the people shapes. They will represent the past million years--ever since people have existed. This is the most recent end of an era when mammals first began to appear, called the "Cenozoic Era."

4. To the left, between 136 and 65 million years—the "Cretaceous Period"—attach the cutout of Tyrannosaurus Rex, Plesiosaurus, Pteranodon, Triceratops, Ankylosaurus, and finally Spinosaurus.

5. Between 193 and 136 million years— the "Jurassic Period"--add first Apatosaurus (Brontosaurus) and then Stegosaurus.

6. Between 225 and 193 million years—the "Triassic Period"—begin attaching turtles and crocodiles and put them all along the time line.

7. Help children notice "who knew whom!" Ask questions such as: *"Who might have known the king of the dinosaurs Tyrannosaurus Rex? Could a turtle have met a Spinosaurus?"*

MEET A DINOSAUR

DINOSAUR FACTS:

● Tyrannosaurus Rex (ty-RAN-o-SAWR-us) "tyrant lizard"; carnivore, walked on two legs with its tail raised up for balance, 39-50' long, 18' tall, teeth 6" long, could dislocate its jaw to eat huge chunks of meat, lived in late Cretaceous Period, bones found in western N. America and China.

What You'll Need:

Tyrannosaurus Rex pattern ● crayons or markers ● collage materials ● glue and sprinkles ● glue ● heavy stock paper ●scissors.

Introduction:

Help children get aquainted withTyrannosaurus Rex. Mix facts with fun art projects. Refer back to the discussion picture on page 9 to talk about the environment in which Tyrannosaurus lived.

What to Do:

1. Give each child a copy of the Dinosaur Pattern. Talk about the name of the dinosaur and some of the facts known about this giant creature.
2. Allow children to personalize their dinosaurs by offering them free use of collage materials.
3. For sturdier results, use the pattern to trace onto folded oaktag for stand up creatures that can be used in skits or in diorama displays.

Challenge:

● Have children cut out their decorated Tyrannosauruses. Demonstrate and then let children put them on the time line in a vertical line in the appropriate place.

Making Connections:

● BEAN BAG TOSS: Cut out one Tyrannosaurus Rex pattern. Place on an overhead projector and enlarge the image onto craft paper. Trace, cut out, and place a poster-sized dinosaur onto the floor. Let each child, in turn, toss a bean bag onto the dinosaur. Have the child name the dinosaur's body part where the bean bag landed. Let him show the others his own corresponding body part.

Books and Resources:

Dinosaurs by Daniel Cohen (Doubleday) A non-fiction book filled with full-color accurate renderings of dinosaurs.
Tyrannosaurus Was a Beast by Jack Prelutsky (Greenwillow) A delightful collection of funny poems.

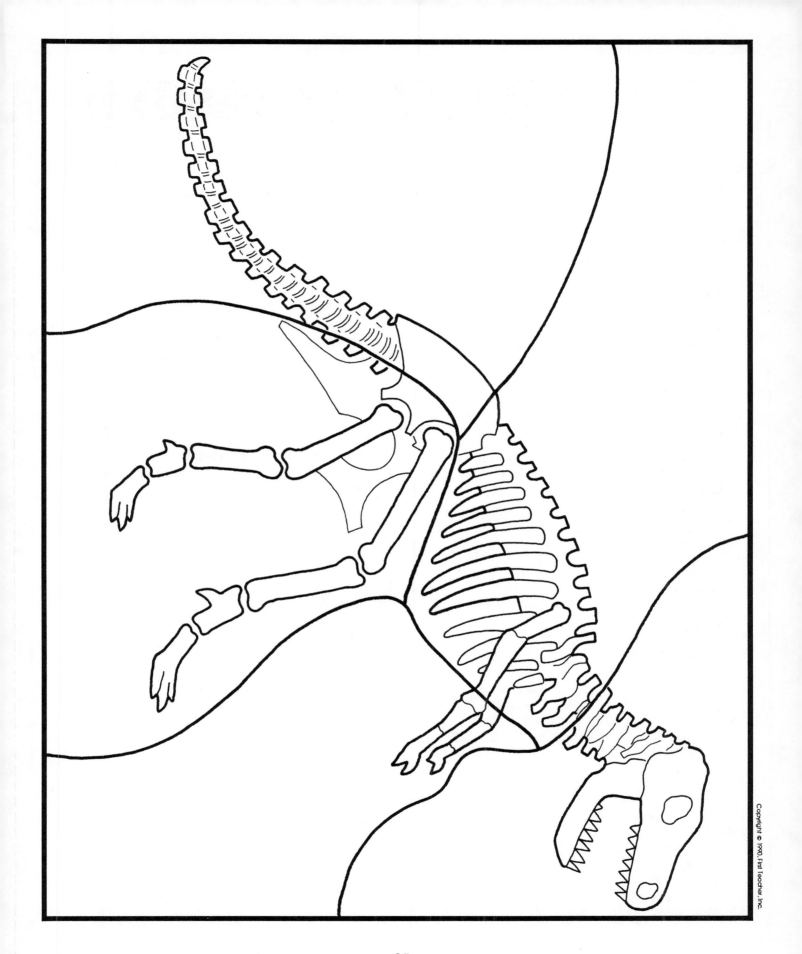

SKELETONS AND FOSSILS

DINOSAUR FACTS:

● "Paleontologists" (PALE-ee-on-TAWL-o-jists) study "the fossil-ized remains of dinosaurs. "Ichnology" (ick-NAWL-o-jee) is the study of fossilized footprints.

What You'll Need:

Copies of page 15 ● scissors ● envelopes ● objects, bones, or dinosaur models ● real fossils (optional).

Introduction:

Show children some prints (previously made in clay or mud) of simple objects. Ask, *"What object made this print?"* Use familiar objects such as a comb, key, toothpick, or spoon; natural items such as acorns, cones, leaves, shells, or tree bark; or clean, dry chicken or turkey bones. Point out that scientists learned what they know about dinosaurs by "reading fossil pictures." If possible, show the class some real rocks with fossils.

Talk about how scientists find parts of dino-saurs fossilized, not the whole creature. These parts present a puzzle for scientists to piece to-gether in order to have an idea of what a whole dinosaur looked like.

What to Do:

1. Give each child a copy of the dinosaur skeleton. Have scissors available.
2. Tell children that this is the skeleton (bones) of the Tyrannosaurus Rex that they just stud-ied. Remind them that scientists did not find these bones all together as in the picture but rather in a different places at different times.
3. Challenge children to make a puzzle out of their dinosaur skeleton. Have children cut along the heavy lines on the Activity Sheet, creating a puzzle. Give each child an en-velope in which to store the puzzle pieces. Have children try to put together their puzzles. Make sure an uncut copy of the

skeleton is available on which children can reassemble the puzzles.

Challenge:

● FOOTPRINTS: If a dinosaur walked in the mud, what kind of footprint would it leave? Provide flat pans of mud, clay, wet sand, play dough, or snow (or work outside where soil and water are available). Have children make their own prints in the materials, then challenge them to use their feet, arms, hands, fingers, or thumbs to create their own version of dinosaur footprints.

Making Connections:

● LAVA'S COMIN': When the dinosaurs died, their bodies were covered with vol-canic lava (melted rock that flows out of volcanos). In this game, half the group be-comes the lava from an explosive volcano. Each of these children has a scarf (the lava). As the dinosaurs are grazing, the volcano leader shouts, "Lava's comin'". The lava group attempts to cover the dinosaurs with the scarves. As soon as a dinosaur is even partially covered with "lava," he becomes a "fossil," and must stay perfectly still.

Books and Resources:

Digging Up Dinosaurs and *Dinosaur Bones* by Aliki (Thomas Crowell). Excellent children's books on fossils!

DINOSAUR PUPPETS

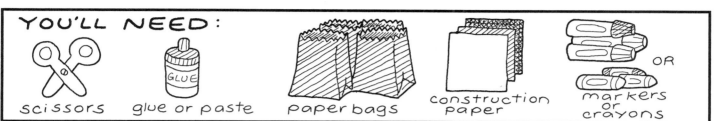

YOU'LL NEED:

scissors · glue or paste · paper bags · construction paper · OR · markers or crayons

MEAT EATERS ☆

TYRANNOSAURUS REX

SPINOSAURUS

PLANT EATERS ☆

APATOSAURUS

STEGOSAURUS

☆ NOT DRAWN TO SCALE

WHAT TO DO:

 1.

Cut and paste TRIANGLE shaped teeth in some puppets. These puppets will be the MEAT EATERS.

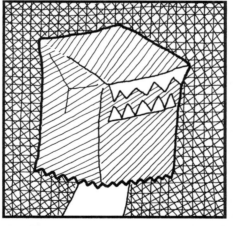

 2.

Cut and paste horizontal RECTANGLE shaped teeth in other puppets. These puppets will be the PLANT EATERS.

 3.

Add features to both groups of puppets: eyes, scales, tails, etc.

MEAT EATER

PLANT EATER

MEAT EATERS AND PLANT EATERS

DINOSAUR FACTS:
● Carnivores ate meat, and usually had sharp, tearing teeth. Herbivores ate plants, and usually had flat, chewing teeth.

What You'll Need:
Paper bag or sock dinosaur puppets: meat and plant eaters (see page 17 for directions)
• small toy animals • small toy vegetables
• paper bag.

Introduction:
The shape and position of the dinosaur's teeth are key to helping scientists decide whether a dinosaur was a meat or plant eater. Help children compare teeth to determine food sources. Suggest that they look at the teeth of present day meat eaters (dogs) and plant eaters (rabbits) in books or live examples.

What to Do:
1. Help children make the puppets described on page 17. Have children choose to make either a meat or plant eater and create the appropriate set of teeth.
2. Gather some toy animals (meat) from a farm set and some toy vegetables (plants) from a kitchen or grocery store set. Place all the items in a large paper bag.
3. Have children make their dinosaur puppets reach in and grab one item with their mouths, pulling it out of the bag. If the proper type of food for that dinosaur is caught, the dinosaur's puppeteer keeps the food. If the dinosaur catches the wrong food, he spits it out!

Challenge:
● FEED THE DINOSAURS: Tape a large picture of a meat eating dinosaur to one side of a clean trash can, and a picture of a plant eating dinosaur to the other side. Give children small plastic plant and animal food sources, and let them take turns trying to "feed" the dinosaur. Have them line up away from the can and toss the correct items into the large dinosaur container (depending on which dinosaur is facing them).

Making Connections:
● TOOTH CARE: Take this opportunity to talk about tooth care with children. Have them look at their own teeth with a hand mirror. Do human teeth look like they would be good for tearing raw meat or eating vegetables? Remind children that we cook our meat and cut it up to make it easier to chew, so even though we are meat eaters, our teeth do not need to be as sharp as a meat-eating dinosaur's did.

Books and Resources:
What Did the Dinosaurs Eat? by Wilda Ross (Coward, McCann & Geoghegan) Story about what the plant-eaters ate.

DON'T BECOME EXTINCT!

DINOSAUR FACTS:
● No one knows for sure why dinosaurs became extinct; there are many theories. The last dinosaurs died about 65 million years ago.

What You'll Need:
Copies of page 19 ● crayons or markers ● scissors ● construction paper ● tissues ● old magazines ● glue ● stapler.

Introduction:
Teaching children health and safety rules is not always an easy task. Young learners are not always interested and many times they fail to understand the importance of practicing accident prevention and good health habits. Incorporating dinosaurs into these lessons is a fun and effective way to teach your children common sense health and safety rules. Talk about the word *extinct*. Tell children that no one knows for sure why there are no more dinosaurs on earth, but many people have ideas. Have children brainstorm their own theories.

What to Do:
1. Give each child a copy of page 19.
2. Have children look at the pictures. Talk about whether the dinosaurs pictured are real or pretend. Tell children that this page shows some silly ways that dinosaurs may have become extinct. Discuss the health or safety issue in each picture.
3. Suggest to children that they use the pictures to make their own Dinosaur Health and Safety Books. Have them color and cut apart the pictures.
4. Have children glue each of the pictures to a piece of construction paper. Help them complete each page as follows:
   ● DANGER: Have children cut out magazine pictures of items they should not touch and glue them on the paper.

● AHH-CHOO: Have children cut out magazine pictures of items—beverages, warm clothes, beds—that could help them recover from a cold. Have them glue these pictures and a tissue on the paper with the appropriate dinosaur scene.
● CAR SAFETY: Have children draw the belt closed over the dinosaur in the picture. Then have them look for car ads in magazines and cut out pictures of cars and seats with seat belts. Have children glue these on the page.
● NOT A TOY: Have children cut out pictures of items they should not play with—matches, sharp scissors, knives, anything electrical—and glue them on the page.
5. Have children staple the pages together to create books.

Challenge:
● POSTERS: Children can make health and safety posters using dinosaurs as the main characters. Brown and Krensky's book described below is an excellent resource.

Making Connections:
● AWARDS: If a child has followed a health or safety rule, award a dinosaur shaped certificate.

Book to Read:
Dinosaurs, Beware! A Safety Guide by Marc Brown and Stephen Krensky (Little Brown) An enjoyable book that offers sixty safety tips for children.

DINOSAUR DICTIONARY

DINOSAUR FACTS:
● Spinosaurus (SPY-no-SAW-rus) "spine lizard" carnivore; walked on two feet; 40-50' long; 20' tall; 4-6 tons; had a "sail" formed by strong spines over 6' high (probably used to regulate body temperature); lived in late Cretaceous Period; bones found in Egypt and Niger.

What You'll Need:
Copies of Dinosaur Pattern cut out • crayons or markers • hole puncher • yarn • glue • strips of paper.

Introduction:
Talking about dinosaurs helps children express themselves and helps them acquire new vocabulary. As children play with dinosaurs, they begin to classify them as the largest, smallest, fastest, slowest, most ferocious, or gentlest. Language continues to expand as imagination takes over and creative thinking emerges.

It won't be necessary to make children memorize dinosaur names or related words. When intrigued, children will learn lots of new vocabulary words on their own: *extinction, climate, fossils, bones, reptiles, mammals, skeletons, lizards,* and *museum.* Give children simple explanations for each unfamiliar word. (The checklist on page 7 might come in handy).

What to Do:
1. Give each child several pre-cut copies of the Dinosaur Pattern.
2. Help children punch two holes in the Patterns and pull yarn through the holes. Tie the yarn to create a booklet.
3. This booklet can serve as a dinosaur dictionary. Let children copy and illustrate new dinosaur vocabulary words they like on the pages of the booklet.

Challenge:
● "THESAURUS": Not only is a Thesaurus a real book, but it also sounds like the name of a dinosaur! This big book can be used to help children learn new words. With the help of a Thesaurus (and an adult), children might choose to tell stories about a huge, enormous, massive, mountainous, gargantuan, immense, or gigantic dinosaur instead of a "big" one. Perhaps the class could create a bulletin board-sized dinosaur named "Thesaurus", using words from the real Thesaurus to describe features, actions, or its life story!

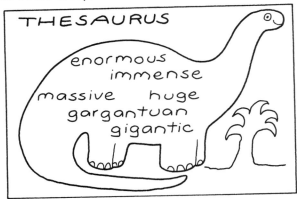

Making Connections:
● WORD OF THE DAY: Have children choose a dinosaur-related descriptive word each day and have everyone try to use that word at least once during the day.

Books and Resources:
Dinosaur Time by Peggy Parish (Trophy) A terrific source of information about dinosaur characteristics and traits.

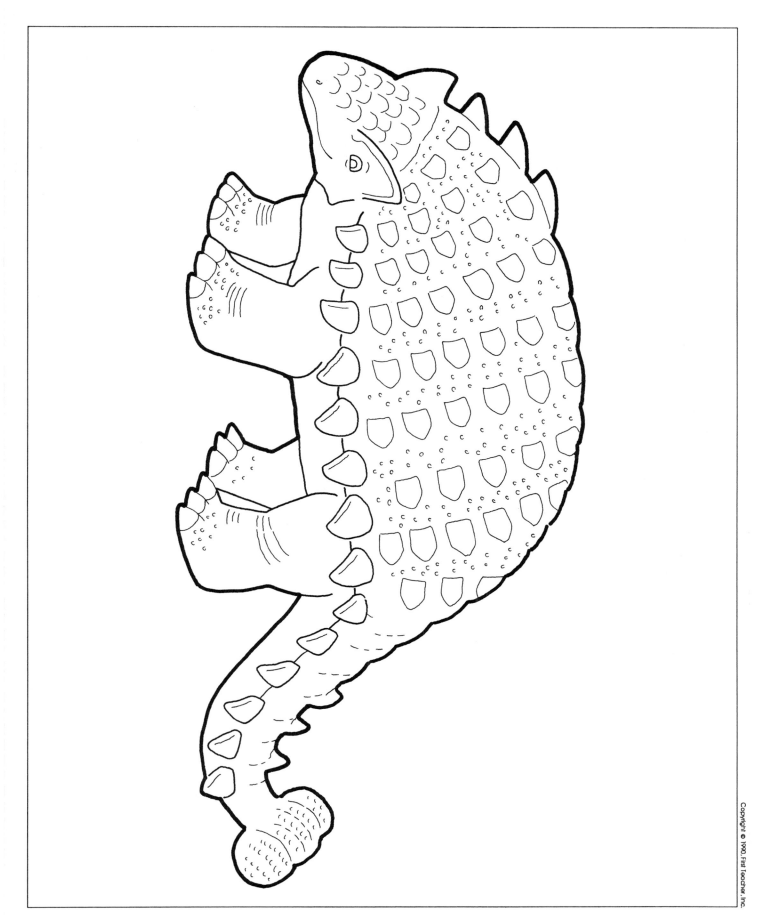

CREATIVE EXPRESSION

DINOSAUR FACTS:
● Ankylosaurus (ANK-kee-lo-sawr-us) or (ank-KILE-o-sawr-us) "fused or stiff lizard"; herbivore; walked on four feet; 15-17' long; 4'-8' tall; covered with heavy armored plates fused with bones; spikes on body; club on tail; lived in late Cretaceous Period; bones found in North America.

What You'll Need:
Large chart paper • tape recorder with blank tapes • Dinosaur Patterns • blank paper • crayons or markers.

Introduction:
To encourage children to create stories, discuss the different kinds of information they could include in their stories:
• what happened (action)
• what the character in the story saw, heard, smelled, tasted, or touched (senses)
• how the character felt (emotions)
Use any well-written fantasy story with a dinosaur theme. As you read the story, note and list on chart paper the words that tell about "actions," "senses," or "emotions."

What to Do:
1. For story starters, ask "What if" questions, such as the following: *"What if you were a dinosaur?" "What if you were visiting in the time of the dinosaurs?" "What if a small dinosaur knocked on your door?" "What if a dinosaur came into our school?"* Use these questions as a stimulus for circletime discussion. Tape record these questions and let children listen to the story ideas at the writing center.
2. Provide children with Dinosaur Patterns and blank paper. Have crayons, pencils, or markers available for children to use as they dictate, scribble write, or use invented spelling to create their own stories.
3. When children have written their own stories, "read" the stories to the class, noting the actions, senses, and emotions in each one.

Challenge:
● STORY PROPS: Create a prop bag or box, including such items as a sweater, a toothbrush, a ball, a hat, and a toy. Challenge each child to take one prop out and tell about how the dinosaur uses it in a story.

Making Connections:
● CLOUD DINOSAURS: Take children outside and help them find dinosaur shapes in the clouds. Together, make up a story about the shapes you see. Since clouds shift quickly, be prepared to change the stories often. Tape record the stories and then transcribe them afterwards. Make these available in the writing center for children to illustrate. (*It Looked Like Spilt Milk* by Charles Shaw (Harper and Row) is a good book to stimulate this kind of creative thinking.)

Books and Resources:
Lost In Dinosaur World, by Geoffrey Williams (Price/Stern/Sloan) Fantasy story and cassette. Great for the listening center. Imagine what it might be like to visit the world of the dinosaurs!

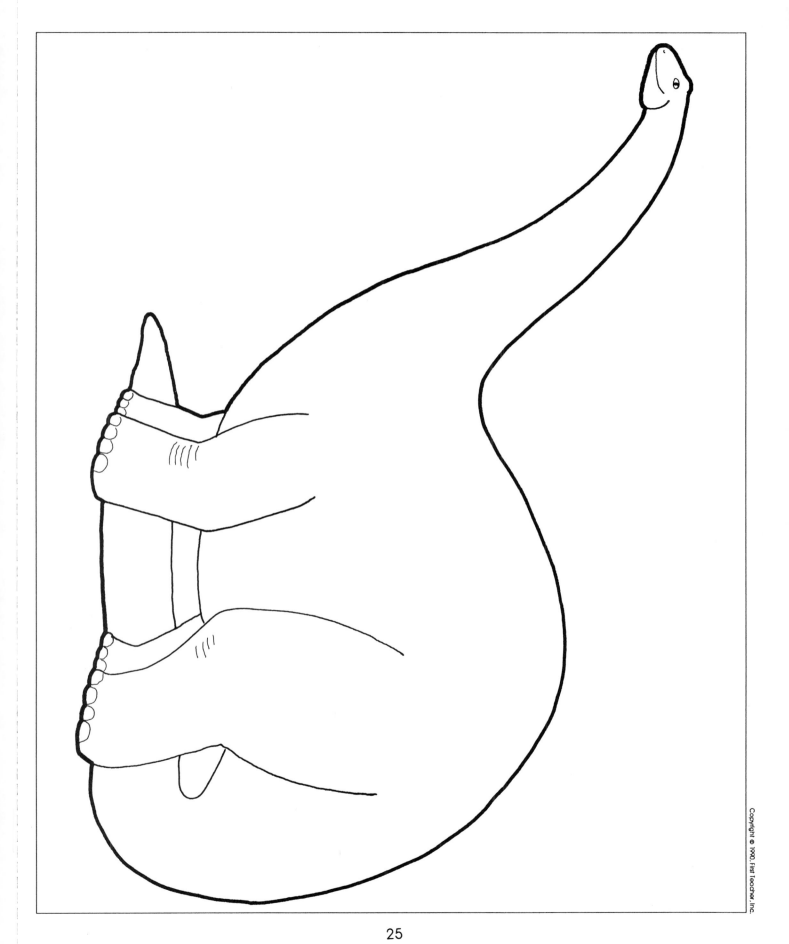

IN THE READING CORNER

DINOSAUR FACTS:
● Apatosaurus (uh-PAT-o-saw-rus) "headless or deceit lizard"; former name: Brontosaurus (bron-tuh-SAWR-us) "thunder lizard"; herbivore; ate needles of conifer trees; walked on four feet; 70' long; 25' tall; 30 tons; feet and legs like modern elephant; small mouth for its huge size; lived during late Jurassic Period; bones found in western U.S.

What You'll Need:
Dinosaur Patterns • crayons or markers • two large baskets • assorted books on dinosaurs • posters • plants • inflated or stuffed dinosaurs.

Introduction:
Children love books. Create an inviting corner where children can explore books about dinosaurs—both fiction and fact-filled books. Give children as many opportunities as possible to deal with fantasy and reality in their play and in books.

What to Do:
1. Have a few children decorate an enlarged Dinosaur Pattern. Help other children print, paint, or cut out the lettering for a sign which says DINO BOOKS.
2. Put two story baskets in the reading area. Look together at your classroom dinosaur book collection. Challenge children to sort the books into the "fiction" or pretend and "non-fiction" or real baskets.
3. Add dinosaur posters, plants, artificial or paper trees for a tropical atmosphere, and large, inflated or stuffed dinosaurs.

Challenge:
● BOOK COVERS: Have children decorate Dinosaur Patterns to use as book covers or title pages for their own dinosaur story books. You may wish to have children create a non-fiction book about a trip to see dinosaurs at a museum. Put children's original books in a special basket in the reading corner for everyone to enjoy.

Making Connections:
● ADD ON STORIES: Read *The Tyrannosaurus Game* by Steven Kroll (Holiday House). Have children make up their own "add on" story. Start it out with something like *"One day we found a very large egg on the playground. As we went over to get a closer look, we heard..."* Let each child add a new part to the story. Write down what each child says on a piece of paper and have the child draw a picture to go with it. Put all these pages together in a class book. Add it to the other books in your reading corner.

Books and Resources:
Apatosaurus by Dave Petersen ("A New True Book," Children's Press) Full of information. Non-fiction.
Going Hollywood by Hudson Talbott (Crown) A rousing tale about change and friendship.

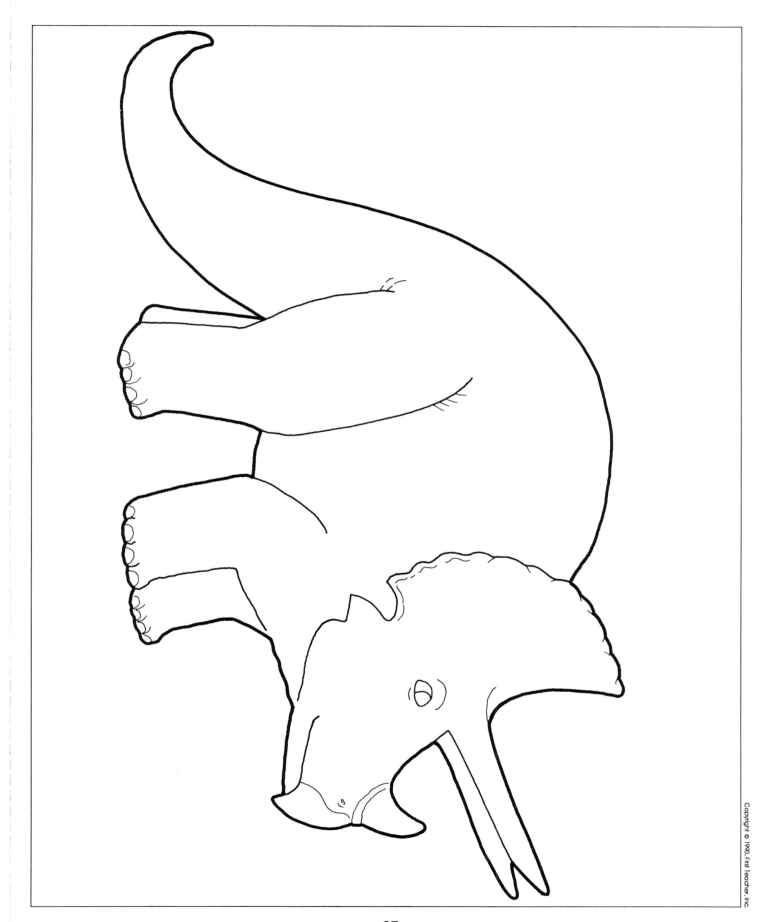

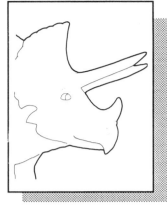

STORIES WITH ACTIVITY IDEAS

DINOSAUR FACTS:
● Triceratops (try-SARA-tops) "three-horned face"; herbivore; walked on four feet; 36' long; 10' tall; 8 tons; massive head, one quarter of his body; bony neck shield (frill); beak-like snout; lived during late Cretaceous Period; bones found in western North America.

What You'll Need:
Baby Triceratops by Beth Spanjian (Longmeadow Press) • Triceratops pattern • crayons or markers.

Introduction:
There are many fictional books that can spark the imagination of children. After reading a book to the class, use a related activity that goes along with the story. Here is an example.

What to Do:
1. Read *Baby Triceratops* to children. This book tells the story of what life is like for a baby Triceratops and its family.
2. After becoming familiar with the story, ask children to retell it in sequence in their own words.
3. Challenge children to add to the story a simple, perhaps silly, dialogue between members of the Triceratops family.
4. Give children several copies of the Triceratops pattern and have them create a Triceratops family, giving special features and a name to each member.

Challenge:
● DINO-MOVIE: Rent a copy of the movie video *The Land Before Time* (Universal). Show the video and talk about the baby dinosaurs in the movie and their search for their parents. Challenge children to create a billboard poster advertising this movie. Let children use Dinosaur Patterns to illustrate parts of the story. Help children think up some exciting words to describe the story.

Making Connections:
Here is a variety of dinosaur-related fictional books with activities to stimulate young imaginations.
● *Danny And The Dinosaur* by Syd Hoff (Harper and Row) Pre-schoolers love to listen to the playful adventures of the dinosaur who came to life when Danny visits a museum.

After reading this book to children, ask them this question: *"If you had a dinosaur for a pet, how would you play with it?"* Write children's dictated answers in the form of a chart story, or make them into a book or a journal. "Interview" children individually and tape record their stories for the entire class to enjoy. Let children think of songs about Danny or dinosaurs. Here is an example. (Tune: Frere Jacques)
Where is Danny? (Repeat)
Here I am. (Repeat)
Playing with a dinosaur, (Repeat)
Having fun. (Repeat)
● *Desmond the Dinosaur* by Althea (Rourke Publications) A story about a shy, little dinosaur who wants to make friends.

Encourage children to use a stuffed dinosaur to pretend they are introducing Desmond to some of their friends. Here is a good opportunity to tie in good manners and making introductions.

● *Dinosaur Bob* by William Joyce (Harper and Row) The Lazardo family brings home an unusual souvenir from their African vacation. Their friendly dinosaur becomes the talk of the town! Bob is the family's pal who can blow a trumpet, dance, and play in a baseball game. Children love this imaginary story that seems very real.

Challenge children's creative thoughts by asking them these questions: *"If you had a dinosaur, where could it take you?" "What might happen if a dinosaur actually showed up at school today?" "If your family had a pet dinosaur, what would you teach it to do?"*

● *Dinosaur Day* and *Dinosaurs' Halloween* by Liza Donnelly (Scholastic) Two imaginative books that invite children to talk about what is happening in the pictures. *Dinosaur Day* is about a boy and his dog who are crazy about dinosaurs. They go dinosaur hunting in their neighborhood and see one under every pile of snow, or so it seems! The boy and his dog are back again in *Dinosaurs' Halloween*. This time they go trick or treating dressed as dinosaurs and meet a small, masked dinosaur who joins them going house to house.

Let children put on their "imagination" hats to be creative about the following questions: *"What might happen if there was a dinosaur on your front porch? Asleep in your back-yard? In your attic?"*

● *Dinosaurs Divorce* by Marc and Laurene Brown (Atlantic) When dinosaur children find that their parents are divorcing, they go through the same feelings as human children do. This book uses cute cartoon-like characters to deal with an important issue.

Let children make dinosaurs with play dough and dino-shaped cookie cutters. Invite children to make "feelings" faces on the dinosaurs using toothpicks. Ask the question: *"How did dinosaur children in the story feel?"*

● *Dinosaur Dos and Don'ts* by Jean Burt Polhamus (Prentice Hall) A book of rhyme that children really enjoy.

Expose children to many of the poems in this book. Then help them create some poems of their own. Using a basic fingerplay rhythm makes it a little easier.

Children may also wish to make up songs. Here is a song to sing about dinosaurs set to a familiar tune. (Tune: Teddy Bear, Teddy Bear)

> *Dinosaur, dinosaur, turn around*
> *Dinosaur, dinosaur, touch the ground*
> *Dinosaur, dinosaur, climb the stairs*
> *Dinosaur, dinosaur, say your prayers*
> *Dinosaur, dinosaur, turn out the light*
> *Dinosaur, dinosaur, say "Goodnight."*

● *If a Dinosaur Came to Dinner* by Jane Belk Moncure (The Child's World) A little boy pretends that a dinosaur comes home with him from the museum. He tells about everything he does with his dinosaur.

Purchase or borrow several stuffed toy dinosaurs. Let children take turns taking them home overnight. The next day encourage children to relate some real and imaginary experiences they had with their dinosaurs.

● *If the Dinosaurs Came Back* by Bernard Most (Harcourt Brace and Jovanovich) This story is about a boy who wishes that wild-colored dinosaurs would come back to earth. It describes how friendly dinosaurs could help people. For instance, they could rescue kites stuck in very tall trees.

Ask children, *"What could a friendly dinosaur do for you?"* Be prepared for a lively discussion.

● *What Happened to Patrick's Dinosaurs?* by Carol Carrick (Ticknor & Fields) In this story, dinosaurs build houses, cars, roads, and airplanes for people. But when the people are only interested in lunch and recess, the dinosaurs leave earth and people have to take care of themselves, but they do not know how. With its wonderful illustrations, this book can be used to demonstrate to children how important it is to be responsible.

● *Prehistoric Pinkerton* by Steven Kellogg (Dial) Pinkerton the oversized pooch, is teething so nothing chewable is safe. When his young mistress takes him on a tour of the museum, will Pinkerton be able to resist a Diplodocus bone?

Help children notice the dinosaur costumes the children are wearing in this story. Cut two pieces of heavy wrapping paper (a dino color), about 30" square. Help children spread glue all over the back of one sheet and put the second sheet on top of it, so both sides are colored. Before it dries, place the sheets on a child's head, and stretch a terrycloth headband over the paper and the head, like a hatband. Leave in place for about 20 minutes, then remove and set aside to dry into a hat shape. Have children add special features (plates, teeth, horns, armor) with fabric, pom-poms, paper plates, felt, and heavy paper to turn these hats into dinosaurs!

DINOSAUR HATS

Ⓐ 2 PIECES OF WRAPPING PAPER — GLUE

Ⓑ TERRYCLOTH HEAD BAND Ⓒ DRY HAT

Ⓓ IDEAS:

HAT FELT "PLATES" ON FABRIC STRIP

POM-POM EYES PAPER TEETH

DINOSAUR FACTS:
- Plesiosaurus (plee-zee-uh-SAWR-us) "Ribbon reptile"; NOT a dinosaur; fat bodied, long-necked reptile; lived in the seas; swam with four flipper-like legs; sharp teeth; ate fish; lived during late Cretaceous Period.

What You'll Need:
Copies of page 31 • crayons or markers • scissors • envelopes.

Introduction:
Because it is not known what sounds dinosaurs made, open the doors of imagination and let children suggest possible noises they may have made! Use creative drama/movement cards to stimulate children's imaginations. The possibilities for children to fabricate stories through movement or mime while creating dinosaur sounds are endless.

What to Do:
1. Give each child a copy of page 31. Talk about the creatures pictured on the Activity Sheet. Clockwise from the top left, the animals are: a Pteranodon (information on page 7), a Tyrannosaurus Rex (page 14), Plesiosaurus (above), Apatosaurus (page 26), Stegosaurus (page 40), Triceratops (page 28). If they wish, let children color the creatures.
2. Have children cut apart the creatures (on the heavy lines). Give children envelopes in which to store their dramatic-play cards.
3. Let children choose cards to act out for the group, making the sounds and movements in the way they believe that prehistoric creature would have done.

Challenge:
- TIME MACHINE: Help children convert a large appliance box into a time machine so they can go back to the days of the dinosaurs. Be sure that they include enough dials, gauges, and levers in the machine for all. When you arrive in dinosaur land, get children started by saying, *"We're here. Step out carefully. Look, a sandy beach. Dip your feet into the ocean. How does the water feel? Can you walk into it? Do you see any trees and plants? What do they look like? What is that loud crashing sound...?"*
- DINO WALK: Help children imagine the sound of a dinosaur walking. Use dowels tapping the floor to represent the dinosaur's feet. Use two dowels for a dinosaur that walked on hind feet (Tyrannosaurus Rex); use four dowels for one that walked on all four feet (Apatosaurus). Have children close their eyes and see if they can hear two or four-legged walking.

Making Connections:
- DINOSAUR MAT: Have a small group of children get on their hands and knees. Place a gym mat over the group and have children move the mat to create a many-legged dinosaur. Encourage the "dinosaur" to try moving back and forth and to walk to a pretend watering hole.

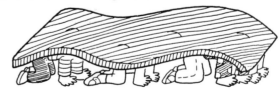

Books and Resources:
- *There's A Dinosaur In The Park* by Rodney Martin (Gareth Stevens) A story about a small boy's imagination. The boy conjures up a large beast in the park.

What to Include in your Math Center:

Dinosaur counting books or pictures • sets of toy dinosaurs (various sizes, and types) • egg carton, with each section numbered 1-12 • sets of clean, boiled turkey or chicken bones (78) • commercial dinosaur skeleton models • dinosaur lotto cards • rulers or "child-osaurus" footprints for measuring.

Introduction:

Logical thinking and math skills are the result of an active child working through exploration with the things in his immediate environment. Children learn about the mathematics of size, shape, seriation, one-to-one correspondence, sets, measurement, numerical recognition, and counting through first hand, tactile experiences with objects. They also learn through carefully planned challenges that promote more abstract thinking skills. Put some dinosaurs in his immediate environment, and the child becomes eager and motivated!

Counting Activities:

● COUNTING CARTON: Number the sections of an egg carton 1-12. Provide a container for several sets of boiled, clean turkey or chicken bones (Warn children not to put the bones in their mouths.)—you'll need a total of 78 bones. Have children count out the correct number of bones for each corresponding egg carton section. Help children separate the bones into subsets of like shapes or sizes and then count the totals in each set they create.

● NUMBER BOOK: Make dinosaur number books using sponge prints of dinosaur shapes or dinosaur footprints, dino stickers, or pictures. Page one has the number one and one dinosaur footprint. Page two has the number two and two dinosaur footprints, and so on.

● DINO SNACK TIME: Make a copy of each of the dinosaur patterns in this book on oaktag or make your own cards and number them 1 to 6. At snack time, have one child randomly choose a number card. Then have children take from the basket for their snack that number of small crackers, raisins, etc., counting them one by one. You can also challenge children or a teacher to cut the whole snack into that chosen number of pieces. As more of a number challenge, ask, *"If you have three crackers each, and the number for the day is 6, how can you break the crackers so there are six pieces?"*

● CONSTRUCTION CREW: Help children make a dinosaur counting zoo. Ask children to build ten "environments" out of construction materials in your class, such as Lego-type bricks, blocks, table cubes, and so on. Then put a number on a card next to each cage. Challenge children to use small dinosaur figures or dinosaur picture cards and place the correct number of the same kind of dinosaurs in each environment.

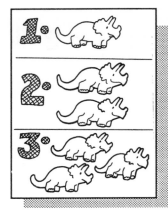

Reasoning Activities:

● SORTING: Let children classify a collection of toy dinosaurs into groups by deciding whether they would walk on two legs or four legs. Help them count the members of each subset. Then have children resort the whole collection into groups of like dinosaurs, such as putting all Stegosauruses together. Ask children to tell in what other ways this group of dinosaurs can be sorted.

Have each child bring a toy dinosaur, book or related item for "show and tell." Help children discuss the shapes, colors, numbers, and sizes in the items shown.

Measurement Activities:

● FOOTPRINTS: Help each child trace around her foot and cut out the print. Have children write their names on the print and add the letters "osaurus." Have children use the footprints to measure various lengths in the room, such as a table, the distance from one end of the room to the other, and the length of the piano. Have children decide how they would use the prints to measure heights.

Activities with Relationships:

● DINO SIZES: Most pre-schoolers know that some dinosaurs were very large. Help children "see" dinosaur sizes by comparing them to everyday things. Explain, for example, that the teeth of Tyrannosaurus Rex were the size of a banana; Apatosaurus (Brontosaurus) was as long as a train car; Ankylosaurus was the size of a big car; and others, like Compsognathus, were only the size of chickens.

Shapes Activities:

● SHAPE DINO: Provide children with geometric shape templates and construction paper. Let them work together in small groups, tracing and cutting out these shapes. Have each group arrange its shapes to create a "shape dinosaur" on mural paper. Encourage children to ensure that their dinosaur has the essential body parts—head, body, legs, and tail. Children may also want to include ears, horns, and plates. When children like their design, help them secure the shapes in place with glue.

● "MATCH THE SHAPE" DINO FAMILY: Use the Dinosaur Patterns to make an assortment of dinosaur families out of felt for the flannel board. Make shapes of felt scraps and glue them onto the dinosaur. Be sure that each dinosaur from the same family has a set of the same shape spots. Make "shape flowers" out of felt with thin rectangular green stems. Use only one type of shape for each flower. Give children opportunities to play at the flannel board. Suggest that a dinosaur with square spots only eats square-shaped flowers and see how well they can match dinos and flowers.

Books and Resources:

Count A Saurus by Nancy Blumenthal (Four Winds Press) A rhyming counting book with an irresistible line-up of Robert Jay Kauffman's colorful prehistoric beasts.

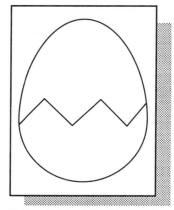

MATH AND DINOSAUR EGGS

DINOSAUR FACTS:
● While it is believed that many dinosaurs laid eggs, there is now some evidence to suggest that some dinosaurs were born alive—Apatosaurus is one that may fit in this category.

What You'll Need:
Copies of page 35 • scissors • crayons or markers • dinosaur stickers (optional).

Introduction:
Bring in a chicken egg and talk about it. Ask questions such as: "Where does it come from? What comes out of it?" Tell children what is known about dinosaur births. Then help children to create a dinosaur egg numbers puzzle.

What to Do:
1. Give each child a copy of page 35. Have crayons or markers and scissors available. You also may wish to use dinosaur stickers.
2. Help each child write a number from one to ten in the top half of the egg. Help children glue or draw small pictures in the bottom to show how many that number represents.
3. Help children cut out their eggs and then cut the eggs in half along the thick jagged line.
4. Mix up the egg halves. Let children put them back together again matching the number half with the half showing the correct number of dinosaurs.

Challenge:
● WHAT'S MISSING?: Arrange one complete set of eggs made above with the numbers in order from one to ten. Remove both halves of one whole egg. Ask children to discover which numbered dinosaur egg has become "extinct."

Making Connections:
● ALL IN ORDER (Seriation): Give children a modeling compound and ask them to make several dinosaur "eggs" and nests of various sizes. Collect them and have children arrange them from smallest to largest or longest to shortest. Let children order model dinosaur figures similarly. Have them arrange eggs with corresponding size differences in front of the creatures.

● HATCH THE DINO EGG: Draw a large oval egg on heavy white paper. Let each child help decorate it. Cut it into two halves and secure these at one corner with a fastener. Talk about what kind of imaginary dinosaur could be inside the egg. Ask, "Will it have horns?" "Should it have a long neck?"

Write down the descriptions as children dictate them. Then as a group, draw and decorate the creature. Attach it behind one half so that when the egg is opened, the creature appears. Use Dinosaur Patterns or let children draw their own baby dinosaurs curled up inside the huge pretend "egg."

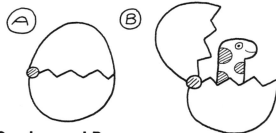

Books and Resources:
● *The Baby Uggs Are Hatching* by Jack Prelutsky (Greenwillow) Cute poems about uggs, sneepies, and slitches!

Introduction:

The dinosaur theme lends itself well to numerous expressions of creativity through art. Once they become familiar with the animals, young children will be able to express their ideas using a wide variety of media. Making lots of different materials available will provide unlimited opportunities for creative expression. Incorporate dinosaurs into both two- and three-dimensional projects, either fanciful creations or realistic ones.

Heavy cardboard dinosaur cut-outs can be used for crayon rubbings, spatter paint art, straw-blown paint designs, water-colored dinos, tissue-paper collage, or finger-painted dinos. Use the dinosaur shapes as a basic design for any art project!

Art Activities:

● DINO T-SHIRTS: Ask parents to send in old T-shirts. Help children decorate them with dinosaurs. Let children use sponges cut into dinosaur shapes or use stencils. Provide fabric paint, fabric crayons, or permanent markers. Be sure children insert folded newspapers between layers of the shirt so the paint or markers do not soak through.

● DINOSAUR MURAL: Have children paint a mural background on newspapers with bright tempera or fluorescent paints. Show them how to leave a two-inch section of the newsprint around the edges for a frame. After the mural is dry, have children add dinosaurs they have made.

● DINOSAUR STAMPS: From thin sponges or foam rug pad scraps, cut dinosaur shapes. Make available thinned tempera paint on shallow plates or provide ink pads. Let children use the shapes to decorate dinosaur book covers, make note cards, form a border for a bulletin board, or add to murals or individual pictures.

● MAKE A DINO MODEL: Let children make free-standing models of dinosaurs from salt/ flour play dough or clay. Provide triangular cardboard, shells, pieces of pasta, toothpicks, pebbles, or pipe cleaners so children can turn their models into more realistic dinosaurs with plates, horns, spikes, armor, teeth, beaks, and other frills.

● DINOSAUR PLAQUE: Try to find dinosaur cookie cutters. Let children use them to cut animals from play dough. Help them put a small hole through the dough at the top. Have children sun dry the cutouts and paint them with small paintbrushes. Point out that their objects will make nice tree ornaments, window hangings, or plaques.

● MAKE A FOSSIL: Provide soft clay. Have children press a leaf, shell, or other object into the clay, and then carefully pull it away. Point out that an impression will remain. Show children how to paint the clay with a little water to moisten it, and then fill the hollow with pre-mixed plaster of Paris. Explain thay they must let the plaster dry. Have them peel off the clay carefully. Show them how to paint their casts, if desired.

● WACKY DINOS: Provide opportunities for children to combine media for 3-D effects. Make available materials such as: styrofoam shapes, toothpicks, cardboard tubes, wire, pipe cleaners, collage scraps, and clay (small wads can be used to stick things together). Invite children to "invent new dinosaurs" by using the materials in any way they want.

● **ACTIVE DIORAMA:** Have children make dioramas showing the types of terrain found where dinosaurs might have lived. Help them set up a table top environment. Provide them with three-dimensional, hand-made or commercial dinosaurs. Have children add some of the following—twigs, ferns, or sprigs standing up in a wad of clay, and clay volcanoes. Show children how to make the volcano by building clay around an empty tin can to which you add one-quarter cup baking soda. Mix one-quarter cup vinegar, one-half cup water with red food coloring, and one-quarter cup dishwashing liquid in a pitcher. Pour the liquid into the can to create an eruption.

● **STUFFED DINO:** Trace and cut double dinosaur shapes from large sheets of heavy paper or furry fabric or let children do so if they can. Let children decorate the dinosaurs. Help children staple or sew the two pieces together, leaving an open area on the side so stuffing can be inserted. Children can do most of the work themselves if heavy paper and yarn are used, and if holes are punched around the outside. Prepare yarn by wrapping one end with a tiny piece of tape to make it into a needle. You may wish to let children use a plastic, blunt-end yarn needle. Before children stuff, have them paint or add texture on the outside with sequins, buttons, or stickers. Help them softly stuff the dinosaurs with wadded tissue or small strips of newspaper and staple or sew the opening. Hang the dinosaurs from the ceiling, staple them to the bulletin board, or let children march them around the room!

● **SHIMMERY DINOS:** Help children cut dinosaur patterns from oaktag. Have them spread a mixture of white glue and water on the patterns. Show them how to sprinkle salt on the dinos so they have a shimmery, reptilian look. Let children color the salt with food coloring if they desire. Children can also paint over the salted dinosaurs with watercolors.

● **STAND-UP DINOS:** Fold a piece of tag board, and trace a dinosaur pattern on both sides. Decorate as desired. Show the children how to cut the double pattern out <u>without</u> cutting on the fold. Then, when cut out, the dinosaur will stand, and can be used in the block or sand area, on a table display, or in a diorama.

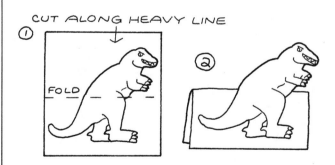

CUT ALONG HEAVY LINE

① FOLD

②

Books and Resources:

● *Dandy Dinosaurs* by Better Homes and Gardens (Meredith Corp) Great resource for craft ideas, recipes, and dino fun!

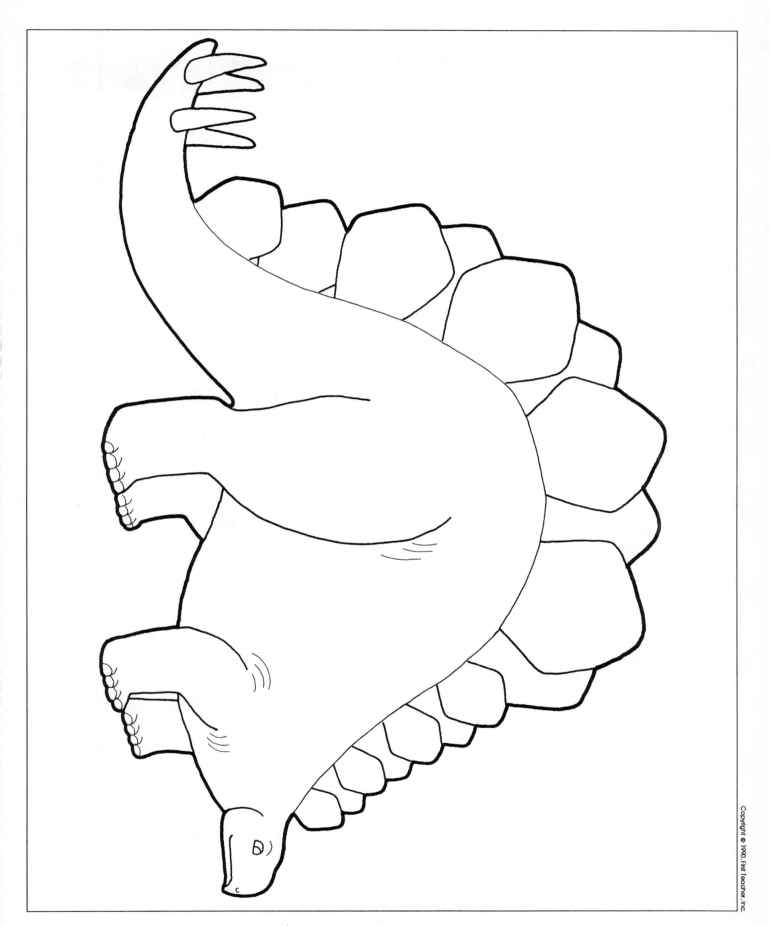

DINO CRAFTS

DINOSAUR FACTS:
• Stegosaurus (steg-o-SAW-rus) "shingle lizard" or "roofed reptile"; herbivore; walked on four feet; 29' long, 2 tons; single or double row of plates all along back; beak-like mouth; four spikes on end of the tail; lived during late Jurassic Period; bones found in western United States—Colorado, Utah.

What You'll Need:
Dinosaur Pattern • black markers • assorted art media.

Introduction:
The shape of Stegosaurus is interesting and familiar to many young children. Let children create a patchwork dinosaur using the Stegosaurus Pattern and then experiment with different art media to fill in the shapes with color and texture. This activity will remind children that scientists think that dinosaur skin had many different colors and patterns or textures.

What to Do:
1. Give each child a Dinosaur Pattern. Have black markers and assorted art media available.
2. Help children divide the dinosaur into three to five parts, outlining each part with a black marker.
3. Ask children to fill in the dinosaur parts as though they were part of a patchwork quilt (it might help to have a real quilt or a picture of a quilt on display), making each a different color and design. Encourage children to experiment with different art materials, using paint in one part, crayon in another, and collage materials in another.

Challenge:
• HANDPRINT STEGGIE: Show children how to use thumbprints and outlines of hands to make dinosaurs. The thumb outline can form the tail of a Stegosaurus—with the addition of four sharp spikes on the end of the tail—and

the little finger his small head. The fingers in between can form the plates on the dinosaur's back. Have children add more plates and details with markers.

Making Connections:
• DINOSAUR RING: Cut a Stegosaurus shape with exaggerated pointed plates on its back from a large cardboard box. Cut two small cardboard supports. Cut slits from the top down in the supports. Place the dinosaur in the slits so it can stand up. Give children rings to toss at "Steggie." Make a picture of Steggie so each child can make a tallymark to show which part was ringed. At the end, let children decide which part was ringed the most and which the least.
• GIANT DINOS: Use an overhead projector to enlarge animals and other shapes to giant size. Let children decide which objects make the best outlines. Ask them to help trace the shapes on butcher paper. Have children cut out and decorate the forms with paint, collage scraps, eggshells, salt or sand textures, or whatever they would like.

Books and Resources:
• *Stegosaurus* by Angela Sheehan (Ray Rourke, Inc.) All about Stegosaurus.

DINOSAUR SONGS AND RHYMES

Below are some songs to sing with children. The children can also make up their own words to these simple tunes.

● PICTURE SONG: Have dinosaur pictures or models available when you sing this song. (The song includes dinosaurs not discussed in this book.) (Tune: "This Old Man")

This dinosaur, he can growl,
(show a meat-eater)
He can growl when he's on the prowl,
(Tyrannosaurus Rex)
With a knick knack, pad-dy whack,
Give your dino a bone.
This dinosaur came growling home.
(Spinosaurus)

This reptile, he can soar,
(show a Pterosaur)
He can soar, but he's not a dinosaur,
(Pteranodon)
With a knick knack, pad-dy whack,
(Rhamphorhynchus)
Give your dino a bone.
This reptile came soaring home.
(Archeopteryx)

This dinosaur, he can walk
(show a plant-eater)
He can walk, but he cannot talk,
(Apatosaurus)
With a knick knack, pad-dy whack,
(Ankylosaurus)
Give your dino a bone.
(Triceratops)
This dinosaur came walking home.
(Stegosaurus)

● OVER THE MOUNTAIN (Tune: "The Bear Went Over the Mountain")

Spinosaurus went over the mountain,
(Repeat two more times)
To see what she could see.
And all that she could see,
(Repeat once more)
Was the other side of the mountain,
The other side of the mountain,
(Repeat once more)
Was all that she could see.

● DINO IN THE DELL (Tune: " The Farmer in the Dell")

Oh, here comes Apatosaurus (or Brontosaurus) (Repeat)
He's called the thunder lizard,
Oh, here comes Apatosaurus.

Let children choose other dinosaurs to sing about. Remind them to substitute the correct nicknames or other words about each one.

● RHYTHM GAME: "Going on a Dinosaur Hunt." This is a seek-and-find game. Have one person hide a collection of plastic dinosaurs and let the others search for them as they sing a variation of the "A Hunting We Will Go" song:

Dinosaur hunting we will go
Dinosaur hunting we will go,
We'll catch a dinosaur and look for more,
And then we'll let them go!

Books and Resources:

● *Dinosaurs* by Lee Bennett Hopkins (Harcourt, Brace, Jovanovich) Beautiful dinosaur poetry that tells lots of information in verse. Try setting these poems to familiar tunes.

VISITING A MUSEUM

A visit to a natural history museum that has a section on dinosaurs provides accurate information for children on what dinosaurs looked like, how they moved, their sizes, what they ate, how they lived, and how they may have died. Museums often have excellent resources such as movies, fossils, books, and models children can see, hear, smell, and touch. Use the museum so children can study its dinosaur skeletons or to get a close look at fossils of various types. Let your museum guide know that you have been discussing dinosaurs and ask to see pertinent exhibits. Use the pre-visit and post-visit activities below to augment what children will learn from the trip!

Before You Go:
● DINO NAME TAGS: Be sure that every child has a personalized dino-shaped name tag. Write the school's name on each. If the class is to be divided into smaller groups, such as one for each chaperone, have each of these groups wear a different dinosaur shape. Take that group's photo in front of the same dinosaur at the museum—when the children find the right one!

Kenny Smith
The Rainbow School

On the Way:
● WHO STOLE THE BONES FROM THE MUSEUM? This game is a rhythmic clapping version of the traditional "Who Stole the Cookie From the Cookie Jar?" Rhythmic patterns of clapping are made with two hands together, clapping one hand with a partner's hand, or slapping thighs. Let children take turns naming different "thieves" of the bones.

Who stole the bones from the museum?
(Lauren) stole the bones from the
museum!
Who me?
Yes, you!
Not me!
Then, who?
(Michael) stole the bones from the
museum!

●READ A STORY: On the way to the museum, read aloud *The Berenstain Bears and the Missing Dinosaur Bone* by Stan and Jan Berenstain (Random House).

At the Museum:
● SCAVENGER HUNT: If you plan ahead, you can have a scavenger hunt with a picture checklist to help children better recognize the names and shapes of the dinosaurs. When chaperones are given just a few children and a checklist, the trip can become much more focused for everyone.
● PARENT FUN: Take paper and markers along so children and parent chaperones can draw their versions of favorite dinosaurs they saw in the museum.

MUSEUM FOLLOW UPS

When You Return:

● TERRARIUM: Discuss what the museum used in their dinosaur background scenes, then help children make a terrarium for a set of small plastic dinosaurs. Provide an old aquarium, a large plastic bowl or a plastic soda bottle with the top cut off. (An overturned glass tumbler over a tiny garden on a pie tin will also work.) Discuss the importance of light, moisture, soil, and temperature in a terrarium. At the bottom of the container, place a piece of plastic screen over a layer of gravel. (This will keep the soil from becoming sour.) Provide potting soil or a mixture of soil, humus, and sand. Let children place the material in the container but explain that it should not be packed tightly. (If you want the terrarium to have a "swampy" look, bring in "muck" from a swampy area! It will sprout and grow water plants.) Let children add moss and tiny cuttings from house plants for quick greenery. Help them water the growths with a spray bottle and cover them with plastic wrap. If too much moisture condenses on the sides of the terrarium, remove the top for a short time. (Some condensation simply indicates adequate moisture in your terrarium.) Indirect light is best.

Books and Resources:

● *My Visit to The Dinosaurs* by Aliki (Crowell) This book explains the history of paleontology, the process of unearthing finds and preparing them for museums. With interesting facts about dinosaur discoveries, the text is simple enough for a four-year-old listener and detailed enough to help teachers learn more about the process of reconstruction.

● *Dinosaurs* by Gail Gibbons (Holiday House) Includes many types of dinosaurs and gives pronunciation guides which are very helpful. Shows how scientists get models in a museum from fossils in the ground. Deals with several theories on why dinosaurs became extinct. The last page on dinosaur footprints is excellent.

● *Dinosaurs, Dragonflies, and Diamonds* by Gail Gibbons (Four Winds) When you take your class to a natural history museum, this book is good to use both for pre-visit and post-visit sharing. It serves to introduce children to the purpose and contents of such wonderful institutions.

● *They Lived With the Dinosaurs* by Russell Freedman (Holiday) With nice black and white photos, this book shows us what types of fossils and animals existed at the same time as the dinosaur, including today's starfish, dragonflies, and sharks!

DINOSAUR DAY

Whatever form your dinosaur unit takes, be sure to wrap up the project with a celebration! To plan a dinosaur party, draw from other sections of this book, and use your imagination! Invite the children to "Bring a Dinosaur to School" (stuffed animals, models, figures, or books). Each child could make a "collar" for his own dinosaur (with the child's name on it), so no dinosaurs will end up in the Lost and Found!

Learning Centers:

If your classroom is divided into learning centers, plan a few special activities at each one for this special day. For example:
- LARGE MOTOR AREA: Have dinosaur dancing, games, or creative movement like Pin the Tail on Stegosaurus. See page 47 for more ideas.
- DRAMATIC PLAY AREA: Turn it into a dinosaur cave.
- SAND TABLE: Hide dinosaur model bones and go on a dinosaur "dig," using small spoons and brushes to carefully wipe the sand away.
- WATER TABLE: Let plastic dinosaurs enjoy bath time!
- MATH AREA: Take a class survey, and map the results onto a graph (types of dinosaurs, colors...).
- SCIENCE AREA: Make plaster casts, dinosaur eggs, or a diorama display.
- ART AREA: Create masks and floats for your dinosaur parade. See page 46 for instructions. Make party hats by stapling Dinosaur Patterns to construction paper headbands.
- COOKING AREA: Make Dinosaur Bread. See page 45 for the recipe.

Routines:

Plan dinosaur-related activities for those routine times that hold the day together. For example:
- STORY TIME: Act out favorite dinosaur stories.
- SNACK TIME: Enjoy a delicious dino-tea party. What would the children's dinosaur friends like to eat and drink? Creative parents or staff can often come up with homemade "dinosaur food" (maybe made with pear halves, bread sticks, raisins, marshmallows, and cut fruit roll-ups). There are now commercial food products shaped like dinosaurs on the market. Roll sugar cookie dough into balls and press into wild dinosaur shapes on a greased cookie sheet. Use raisins for eyes or sprinkle with multi-colored sprinkles or colored sugar. Bake your dinosaurs and serve with "Swamp Tea" (apple juice simmered with cloves and a cinnamon stick, then cooled).

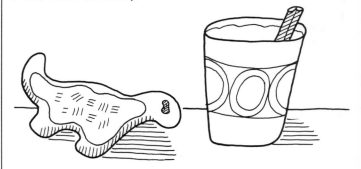

- REST TIME: Finally, and sometimes gratefully, there can even be a "dinosaur rest time" (phew!).
- DEPARTURE: Time for all the dinosaurs to say good-bye and go back "from whence they came"! It was well worth it!

DINOSAUR BREAD

YOU'LL NEED:

 frozen bread dough- thawed

 egg yolk

raisin

water

 paintbrush- for adding glaze

food coloring

 muffin tin

cookie sheet

spray vegetable oil pan coating

WHAT TO DO:

 1.
Give each child a ball of dough. Let children make many small balls.

 2.
Grease a cookie sheet and make an outline of a large apatosaurus on the greased sheet.

 3.
Help children fill in the outline with their many small dough balls. Round up the body with several layers.

 **4.**
Add a raisin for an eye.

 5.
Let dough rise until double, then paint with a glaze of egg yolk mixed with water.

 6.
If you add food coloring to the glaze, the dinosaur will be in color!

 7.
Bake at 325° F - 350° F for 45-50 minutes or until golden brown. The dinosaur will be 3-dimensional and bumpy.

 8.
You could also make large rolls in muffin tins or mix popovers from a mix and call them DINOSAUR EGGS!

A DINOSAUR PARADE

What You'll Need:
Large brown grocery sacks • balloons • paint • crayons or markers • paper • small wheeled toys • crepe paper streamers • stuffed dinosaurs.

Introduction:
Why not have a parade to celebrate all you and your children have learned about dinosaurs? Our directions for masks and floats will help make your parade very festive, but an impromptu version is almost as much fun.

What to Do:
1. Help children make dinosaur masks. To prepare paper sacks for masks, cut eye openings at the top and semi-circles from the bottom to fit comfortably over a child's shoulders. Let children add horns, eyes, and bony collars made from paper plates. Suggest that the masks look like actual dinosaurs or you might say: *"We don't really know what ALL dinosaurs looked like. Let's create our own!"* Encourage children to give their masks expressions that convey how they are feeling. Give them the freedom to create "sadosaurus," "happyosaurus," "grumpyosaurus," or even "jumpyosaurus," in any shape, color, or mood they choose.

2. Help children make "fabulousaurus floats." Have children decorate wheeled toys and wagons with crepe paper streamers or balloons. Use the floats to pull stuffed toy dinosaurs or children wearing dinosaur masks.

3. What's a parade without music? Add dinosaur stickers to simple hand-made musical instruments, (drums from oatmeal boxes, tambourines from small paper plates stapled together with beans inside, and ribbons with bells). Add music, sing, and join the parade! Favorite dinosaur songs are: "Please Don't Bring a Tyrannosaurus Rex to Show and Tell" by Joe Scruggs (*Late, Late Last Night*), and "If I Had A Dinosaur" by Raffi (*More Singable Songs*).

4. Mark your parade route with dinosaur signs so the parade can twist back and forth around the room or hall.

DINOSAUR GAMES

Introduction:

To round out your dinosaur celebration (or for some dinosaur fun any time in the school day), try some of the following game ideas. When cooperative games are offered, they can help reinforce motor skills and coordination without frustration and competition.

Games:

● "THOSE LOVABLE DINOSAURS": Place a group of plastic and stuffed dinosaurs together on the floor. Have one player at a time choose a dinosaur to hug and give a pretend kiss. Let the game continue until each child has had a turn to hold a dinosaur and recite:

> *"One day while walking down the street,*
> *Some lovable dinosaurs I did meet,*
> *One made a sound, just like this,* (have child make up sound)
> *So I took him home and gave him a kiss!"*

● MUSICAL DINOSAURS: Musical Dinosaurs is a cooperative version of musical chairs. Spread a set of dinosaur pictures around on the floor. Play some music and let children move around the floor like dinosaurs. When the music stops, each child "dinosaur" must be on a picture of a dinosaur. The "dinosaurs" not on a picture become "extinct" and cover themselves with "lava"— a scarf or sheet. They rest "for millions of years" until at the end of the game, the last one left alive turns into a paleontologist and uncovers the extinct dinosaurs one by one. Then the game can begin again.

● DINOSAUR RACES: Hold some non-competitive, "I can do it!" races. Clear a place in the room or go outside and mark paths with tape. Give directions such as: *"Walk on four legs like an Apatosaurus. Now stand and stretch tall like a Tyrannosaurus. See if Rex can walk backwards."* Give each child a dinosaur shaped certificate as they finish the circuit. You may wish to incorporate other motor skills into the race such as: rolling, standing on one foot, galloping, skipping, clapping, turning, or touching toes.

● DINOSAUR TRACK RELAY: Divide the class into two groups to play Dinosaur Track Relay. One group is the Apatosaurus group and the other the Tyrannosaurus Rex group. The Apatosaurus walked on all fours with a supportive tail— its print would have five parts. Tyrannosaurus Rex walked upright on two strong hind feet— its print would have two parts. Draw and cut out tracks that correspond to the two dinosaurs. One child from each team has to follow the tracks of its dinosaur to the goal line and back again. When he returns, the next child in line repeats the course. Everyone wins when the course is completed by both teams.

● DINOSAUR STEP: Dinosaur Step is a version of Giant Step. A Tyrannosaurus Rex step is an upright step equal to one large step. The Apatosaurus step is a movement on all fours—each limb moves ahead one step. The leader gives out directions to each player to take a specific number of Tyrannosaurus steps or Apatosaurus steps. The game ends when everyone has reached the leader.

A CLASS DINOSAUR

What You'll Need:
Art media • scissors • glue.

Introduction:
As you near the end of your dinosaur unit, it is time to empower your children with the mightiness of dinosaurs by helping them use all that they have learned to create their own wacky or realistic dinosaurs. Here is a step-by-step plan for your class creation.

What to Do:
1. Call children to a circle time and brainstorm with them about what they would like <u>their</u> dinosaur to be like. They can decide if they want their class dinosaur to be wacky or realistic (totally mythical or somewhat creative, but based on facts). Quickly sketch children's ideas on large easel paper. During the brainstorming session, decide on the following:
   - size of "their" dinosaur
   - weight/height
   - number and length of legs
   - head shape
   - body length and description
   - skin texture
   - temperament (describe its' personality)
   - color(s)
   - wings/plates/armor/scales/frill
   - tail length and description
   - sharp or dull teeth (related to food source)
   - food source (plants or other animals)

2. Help children invent a dinosaur name for their creation. They'll need a name for the type of dinosaur they've created and a name they'd like to call it ("Tom the Giantosaurus").

3. Get the whole class to work together to create one big three-dimensional dinosaur to fit the "group imagination" of what their "invented" dinosaur might look like. Large and small boxes, balls, cardboard tubes, paper bags stuffed with newspaper, fabric, old sheets, wire, pieces of hose, and even balloons can be used to create the biggest dinosaur that can fit in your room (or maybe it won't fit!). You might use a table as a base. Fasten pieces with lots of heavy tape, or hook pieces together with scraps of rope. (Punch a hole in the box or bag, stick one end of the rope through and tie it in a knot so that end can't come back out.) Give it some color with paint or markers, wrap it in crepe paper, or cover big sections with colorful sheets or blankets. Use tape to attach paper eyes, shell scales, or whatever you choose. Nobody will want to miss this project! Be sure to have a camera ready!